# BOOK ANALYSIS

By Sarah Barnett-Benelli

# Sophie's Choice
## BY WILLIAM STYRON

Bright
≡Summaries.com

**BOOK ANALYSIS**

# Shed new light
# on your favorite books with

Bright
≡Summaries.com

**www.brightsummaries.com**

| | |
|---|---|
| **WILLIAM STYRON** | **9** |
| ***SOPHIE'S CHOICE*** | **13** |
| **SUMMARY** | **17** |
| Sophie's story | |
| Meeting with Nathan | |
| **CHARACTER STUDY** | **25** |
| Stingo | |
| Sophie Zawistowska | |
| Nathan Landau | |
| Larry Landau | |
| Morris Fink | |
| **ANALYSIS** | **33** |
| The mature Stingo looks back | |
| Slavery and the South | |
| Counterpoint | |
| **FURTHER REFLECTION** | **43** |
| **FURTHER READING** | **49** |

# WILLIAM STYRON

## AMERICAN NOVELIST, ESSAYIST AND MEMOIRIST

- **Born in Newport News, Virginia, USA in 1925.**
- **Died in Martha's Vineyard, Massachusetts, USA in 2006.**
- **Notable works:**
  - *Lie Down in Darkness* (1951), novel
  - *The Confessions of Nat Turner* (1967), novel
  - *Darkness Visible* (1990), memoir

William Styron was born in Newport News, Virginia in 1925. He served in the US Marines before graduating from Duke University, Durham, North Carolina. During the 1950s he was part of the community of American ex-pats in Paris that included the writers James Baldwin, Peter Mathieson and George Plimpton. The group founded the prestigious quarterly English literary magazine, *The Paris Review*. Styron's first novel, *Lie Down in Darkness*, established him as one of America's most promising young writers and won him the prestigious Rome Prize, which enabled him to study and write in Italy. *The Confessions of Nat Turner,* a fictionalised account of a historic slave rebellion in 1831, won a Pulitzer Prize, but met with controversy for its representation of black people. Styron was a passionate supporter of Civil Rights and an opponent of the war in Vietnam. In 1982 *Sophie's Choice* was made into a feature film for which Meryl Streep, who played Sophie, won an Academy Award.

# *SOPHIE'S CHOICE*

## NOVEL

- **Genre**: novel
- **Reference edition:** Styron, W. (1980) *Sophie's Choice*. London: Corgi.
- **1st edition:** 1979
- **Themes:** slavery, the Holocaust, World War II, domestic violence, guilt, mental health, suicide, sexual frustration

*Sophie's Choice* is a troubling novel that revolves around the character of Sophie, a Polish Catholic, who has a terrible choice to make when she is taken to the Nazi concentration camp at Auschwitz-Birkenau. She survives the war but the mental trauma she suffers afterwards makes her ripe for an abusive relationship with Nathan, a paranoid schizophrenic. The two form an unhealthy co-dependency that leads to their double suicide. The narrator, Stingo, tells Sophie's story within the framework of his own. Stingo is an aspiring writer who is drawn, against his better judgment, into friendship with the couple. He falls in love with Sophie, who confides in him, gradually opening up and revealing the terrible story of what happened to her at Auschwitz-Birkenau.

# SUMMARY

Stingo is 22 years old and an aspiring writer, but since going to work as a junior editor at the publishers McGraw-Hill, he has not been able to write creatively. His job is to read mainly tattered and inferior manuscripts. He rejects them all, including one which later becomes a huge success: *Kon-tiki*. To his relief he is dismissed from his post, but realises he will have to move from his tiny but expensive room in Manhattan to Brooklyn, where property is cheaper. He is helped by a legacy of 484 dollars from the sale of a slave, Artiste, owned by his great-grandfather at the time of the American Civil War (1861-1865).

Stingo finds a large, airy room in a house owned by Yetta Zimmerman. She calls her house "Yetta's Liberty Hall" (p. 50), because the tenants are free to entertain friends of the opposite sex in their rooms. This greatly appeals to Stingo, but he wonders where he will find a girl. Stingo is still a virgin and struggling with sexual frustration. He is hoping for peace and quiet so he can get on with his writing and is distressed by the noise of frenzied lovemaking in the room immediately above his, followed by a violent argument and the sound of a woman sobbing.

Yetta's house is in Flatbush, a mainly Jewish area of Brooklyn. Stingo goes out to lunch at a Jewish restaurant, where he feels very comfortable. Stingo was brought up as a Christian but now considers himself to be agnostic.

On his return he meets Morris Fink, who tells him that the woman in the room above his is Sophie Zawistowska. Her lover is Nathan Landau, whom Morris finds weird. He thinks he is in need of psychiatric help. Morris hands Stingo a letter. It is from his father, who encloses a newspaper clipping about a young woman called Maria Hunt. Maria has committed suicide by jumping from a roof. Stingo is devasted, as he was in love with Maria when he was an adolescent. He falls asleep on his bed and has a terrible nightmare. When he wakes up, he hears the bedsprings creaking again upstairs.

Distressed, Stingo goes out for a walk, and when he comes back he finds Sophie and Nathan arguing beside his door. Nathan is being abusive and Sophie is sobbing and begging Nathan not to leave her. Nathan jeers at Stingo for his Southern accent, implicating him by association with Southern racist prejudices and atrocities, even though Stingo is a liberal thinker. After Nathan has gone, Stingo tries to comfort Sophie and notices a purple tattoo on her arm. He assumes her to be Jewish but she is in fact a Polish Catholic.

Stingo is amazed and angry when the couple appear at his door the next morning and invite him to go to the beach with them. It is obvious there is something seriously wrong with the couple's relationship, but against his better judgment Stingo becomes their friend and the confidant of Sophie, with whom he falls in love.

## SOPHIE'S STORY

Sophie tells Stingo of her early life in Cracow before the war and then of life under the Nazis after the occupation of Poland in 1939. She presents her family as liberal thinkers and says that her father, when young, had hidden three Jewish families during a Russian pogrom. As she grows to trust Stingo, she tells him this was not true, that her father was in fact a fascist and anti-Semite who had written an anti-Semitic pamphlet. As his secretary she was obliged to type this. Her husband was her father's protégé and she hated them both.

After her father and husband were killed, she moved to Warsaw with her mother and two children, Jan and Eva. Her mother was very ill with tuberculosis and she went into the countryside to buy her some meat. This was illegal as any available meat was only for the Nazi soldiers. Sophie is caught and arrested and sent with her children to Auschwitz. When she arrives she is obliged to choose which child should live and which should die – the terrible "Choice" of the novel's title. She chooses her son Jan to live and he is sent to the children's camp, where she is not allowed to see him.

Because of her secretarial skills and perfect command of the German language, she is sent to work at the house of the camp Commandant, Rudolf Franz Höss. She is still a prisoner and wears prison clothes. Like the other prisoners who work in the house, she is fed on leftovers from the family table, some half-chewed, but this is much better than the starvation-level rations given to prisoners in the camp.

She gets to hear of the *Lebensborn* programme, in which children in Nazi-occupied countries who had the right Aryan looks were stripped of their identities and sent to Germany to be brought up by pro-Nazi families. The idea appals her but she would prefer that to happen to Jan than for him to die in the camp, even though she knows she would never see him again.

Realising that Rudolf Höss is attracted to her, she begs him to allow her son to go on the *Lebensborn* programme. She has with her, hidden in the lining of her boot, a copy of her father's anti-Semitic pamphlet. In an attempt to help Jan, she shows Höss the pamphlet and tries to convince him that she herself is an anti-Semite. It does not work. Höss lets her down and she ends up back in the camp.

She nearly dies of starvation but survives the war and is sent to a displaced persons' camp, then on to Brooklyn, New York, where she works for a Polish chiropractor.

## MEETING WITH NATHAN

Sophie's constitution is still weak, and following a nasty sexual assault on a train she becomes very ill. She collapses one day at the Brooklyn College Library and is rescued by Nathan, whom she thinks is a doctor. He takes her to his brother Larry, who really is a doctor and arranges for her to receive treatment for her severe anaemia. Nathan is kind and gentle with her and she falls in love with him. He tells her he is a biologist working on something important. This is not true. Nathan is in fact a paranoid schizophrenic who has a small job at the laboratory's library.

Stingo sees for himself how badly Nathan treats Sophie when he flies into one of his rages, which are exacerbated by his addiction to the drug Benzedrine. Nonetheless, he is stunned when she confides more details of the sadistic beatings she has endured at his hands. Nathan suspects that Sophie and Stingo are having an affair, which is not true, but when Nathan threatens to shoot them both Stingo persuades the terrified Sophie to go with him to his father's inherited peanut farm in Southampton County, Virginia. Stingo is losing touch with reality as he convinces himself that Sophie will marry him and come to live with him on the farm.

They leave by train but get off at Washington for a break and book into a hotel as husband and wife. Stingo is still a virgin, but at Sophie's initiating they make love. Sophie, however, leaves at dawn and goes back to Brooklyn to be with Nathan. When Stingo arrives back at Yetta's house he finds that Nathan and Sophie have killed themselves by taking sodium cyanide. They are lying together on Sophie's bed wearing the costumes they liked to dress up in.

# CHARACTER STUDY

## STINGO

Stingo was born and grew up in Virginia, one of the Southern United States of America. He has no siblings and his mother died when he was 13. In 1943, at the age of 17, he entered the Marine Corps. World War II was in its fifth year, but at this point Stingo knew nothing about the concentration camps, or the systematic destruction of European Jewry by the Nazis. Stingo is an aspiring writer and has started a novel, but is suffering from writer's block. He is still a virgin and struggling with sexual frustration. After losing his job as a junior editor with McGraw-Hill, a job he dislikes, he moves from Manhattan to Brooklyn, where he meets Sophie and Nathan, who are his neighbours in Yetta Zimmerman's rooming house. Nathan mocks him for his Southern accent and implicates him by association in Southern racist atrocities, even though Stingo is in fact a liberal thinker. It is obvious from the beginning that there is something seriously wrong with the couple's relationship, but against his better judgment Stingo becomes their friend and the confidant of Sophie, with whom he falls in love. She gradually opens up her tragic history to a shocked Stingo. 20 years later the mature Stingo, now a successful novelist, begins to think of writing her story, though several years pass before he actually begins.

## SOPHIE ZAWISTOWSKA

Sophie is a Polish Catholic who was born and brought up in Cracow. Her mother was an accomplished pianist and Sophie wanted to study music in Vienna, as her mother had, but the war got in the way of her aspirations. Sophie's father was a professor of law. She was married to his protégé, Kazik Zawistowska, who like him was a fascist and anti-Semite. Her father was controlling and Kazik had the same abusive traits. Like other university professors, they were shot by the Nazis, despite her father's insistence that he shared their anti-Semitic views. Sophie moved to Warsaw with her mother and two children, Jan and Eva, where she was arrested for smuggling fresh meat for her sick mother. She was transported to Auschwitz-Birkenau, along with her children and some friends who had been part of the Polish resistance. Sophie herself had refused to help the resistance because of fears for her children's safety. When they arrived at Auschwitz-Birkenau, she was forced to decide which of her children would live and which would go straight to the gas chamber, the terrible "Choice" of the novel's title. In Brooklyn, Sophie works for Dr Blackstock, a Polish chiropractor. Dr Blackstock is kind to Sophie but Nathan refuses to believe there is nothing sexual between them. Sophie suffers from a profound survivor's guilt because she was not able to save her children and because she posed as a collaborator and anti-Semite in order to try and help Jan. Her guilt turns her into a victim willing to accept the appalling abuse inflicted on her by Nathan.

## NATHAN LANDAU

Nathan Landau comes from a wealthy Jewish family. His father was a Latvian immigrant who had built up a successful business canning kosher soups. His brother Larry is a doctor. Nathan is intelligent and well-read and tells everybody he has a degree from Harvard and is a research biologist at Pfizer's laboratory. This is not true: Nathan has no degree and is a paranoid schizophrenic who over the years has been in and out of psychiatric hospitals. When he was in his late teens, Nathan tried to burn down his parents' house. He has long periods of remission when he is relatively tranquil and does have a job as an assistant in Pfizer's library, a job obtained for him through a contact of his father's. When he is in control of himself he apparently does a good job in the library and occasionally does a little research for one of the legitimate biologists. However, he is very unpredictable and suffers from sudden mood swings, exacerbated by his addiction to the drug Benzedrine. He is very kind to Sophie when they first meet and pays for the medical treatment she needs. He also buys Sophie a phonograph (record-player) and records, so she can play the classical music she loves.

## LARRY LANDAU

Larry, a doctor, is Nathan's brother. When Nathan first meets Sophie in the Brooklyn College Library, she is very ill and he takes her to see Larry. Nathan believes (correctly) that Sophie has severe anaemia and Larry recommends a specialist to treat her. It is Larry who eventually tells Stingo the truth about Nathan. He hopes Stingo will be a positive influence on his brother and discourage him from taking Benzedrine, which makes his condition worse. He also asks Stingo to keep an eye on Nathan and report back if he seems to be going out of control. Stingo agrees to do this but shortly afterwards goes to South Carolina for ten days to visit his old Marine Corps friend, Jack Brown. It is during this period that the events leading up to the final tragedy take place. Afterwards he feels that had he "stayed on the scene during those crucial days", he may well have been able to halt Nathan's "last slide towards ruin", and sees his absence at that time as a "grave dereliction" of duty (pp. 569-70). He also berates himself for not having told Sophie what Larry had told him (*ibid.*).

## MORRIS FINK

Morris Fink is one of the tenants at Yetta Zimmerman's rooming house. He acts as a janitor when Yetta is away and knows everything that is going on there. Morris had lived in what became Stingo's room, but moved to another room because he could not stand the noise from upstairs. It is Morris who tells Stingo who the couple above him are and says he thinks Nathan is in need of psychiatric help (p. 61). When Stingo is in South Carolina visiting Jack Brown, he gets a phone call from Morris Fink telling him that Nathan has "gone off his trolley again" and tried to kill Sophie (p. 582). Morris asks Stingo if he should call the police, but Stingo tells him not to do so (*ibid.*). Stingo tries to ring Larry, but he is away in Toronto.

# ANALYSIS

*Sophie's Choice* is a troubling novel, full of racial tensions and difficult subjects, such as the Nazi Holocaust of World War II, slavery, mental health, suicide and domestic violence. Sophie, and the terrible choice she had to make when she was taken to the concentration camp at Auschwitz-Birkenau, form both the book's title and its central focus.

In the novel we see the horrors of Auschwitz and the extermination camp of Birkenau, not through Jewish eyes but filtered through the experience of a Polish Catholic, Sophie. Unlike the majority of those sent to the concentration camps, Sophie survives, but the mental torment of what she has seen and been forced to do never leaves her. She is devasted that she was unable to save her children and burdened by a terrible guilt at having to choose which of them would live and which would die. She also sees herself as a collaborator, as well as a victim, for the way she used her father's anti-Semitic pamphlet to try and convince the camp commandant that that she too was an anti-Semite and therefore on his side:

> "the word guilt, I discovered that summer, was often in her vocabulary, and it is now clear to me that a hideous sense of guilt always chiefly governed reassessments she was forced to make of her past. I also came to see that she tended to view her own recent history through a filter of self-loathing – apparently not a rare phenomenon among those who had undergone her particular ordeal" (p. 198)

Full of guilt and self-loathing, Sophie falls in love with Nathan, a paranoid schizophrenic who declares his love for her, but falls into jealous rages and beats and abuses her and accuses her of being a whore. In one troubling incident early in the book, Morris Fink tells Stingo that he has seen her lie on Nathan's bedroom floor and wordlessly accept a beating and a kicking (p. 84). Her guilt has turned her into a victim willing to accept the appalling abuse inflicted on her by Nathan.

As the novel goes on Sophie begins to drink heavily, and as the alcohol loosens her tongue she tells Stingo things she has not been able to tell Nathan.

# THE MATURE STINGO LOOKS BACK

The year is 1967. By now Stingo is a successful writer. The book he was struggling with while living at Yetta Zimmerman's house (based on the family of the doomed Maria Hunt) had been published long before, to: "a general acclaim far beyond my youthful hopes" (p 288). His mind is turning to Sophie and Nathan and the tragedy with which he became embroiled in the summer of 1947. He feels this is something he will eventually have to deal with in the same way he dealt with his memories of Maria Hunt, by writing a novel about her.

The mature Stingo is well-read in literature dealing with the Nazi Holocaust. He is interested in the Jewish writer George Steiner's book of essays, *Language of Silence*. Obsessed with knowing precisely what he was doing on April 1, 1943, the day that Sophie entered Auschwitz, Stingo experiences a "shock of recognition" when he reads Steiner's insights on the "time relation" (p. 289), that is the realisation that two vastly different experiences are taking place at precisely the same time. Writing of the brutal killing of two particular Jews at the Treblinka extermination camp, Steiner says:

> "One of the things I cannot grasp, though I have often written about them, trying to get them into some kind of bearable perspective ... is the time relation... Precisely at the same hour in which Mehring and Langner were being done to death, the overwhelming plurality of human beings, two miles ... or five thousand miles away ... were sleeping or eating or going to a film or making love or worrying about the dentist. This is where my imagination balks. The two orders of human experience are so different, so irreconcilable to any common norm of human values, their coexistence is so hideous a paradox ... Are there, as science fiction and Gnostic speculation imply, different species of time in the same world, "good time" and enveloping folds of inhuman time, in which men fall into the hands of the living damnation" (pp. 289-90)

Considering whether he should write the novel at all, Stingo admits to being:

> "haunted by an element of presumption in the sense of being an intruder upon the terrain of an experience so bestial, so inexplicable, so undetachably and rightfully the possession alone of those who suffered and died, or survived it" (ibid.)

Stingo quotes Steiner again: "[it is not clear] that those who were not themselves fully involved should touch upon these tragedies unscathed" (p. 292), and the Jewish Holocaust survivor, Elie Weisel:

> "Novelists made free use of [the Holocaust] in their work... In so doing they cheapened [it], drained it of its substance. The Holocaust was now a hot topic, fashionable, guaranteed to gain attention and to achieve instant success …" (ibid.)

Nonetheless, Stingo decides to risk writing Sophie's story, although a few years will go by before he begins.

## SLAVERY AND THE SOUTH

The history of slavery in the Southern United States is introduced in the second chapter, when Stingo narrates the story of his legacy of 484 dollars that originated in the sale of his paternal great-grandfather's slave, Artiste. It is a sad story: Artiste was wrongly accused of making an improper advance to a young white girl and "sold into the grinding hell of the Georgia Turpentine forests" (p. 47). When his great-grandfather discovered the girl had lied, he tried to find Artiste, but with no success.

When he was a boy, Stingo's grandmother: "a shrunken little doll of an old lady approaching ninety" (p. 40), had told him about the two young slaves she had possessed as a girl of 13:

> "I have often found it a little difficult to believe that I have been linked so closely in time to the Old South, that it was not an earlier generation of my ancestors who owned black people, but there it is: born in 1848, my own grandmother possessed two small negro hand-maidens, only a little younger than herself, regarding them as beloved chattels all through the years of the Civil War, despite Abraham Lincoln and the articles of emancipation" (ibid.)

Stingo's great-grandfather suffered a lot of guilt when he realised that not only had he sold an innocent boy into such a terrible situation, but had committed: "one of the truly unpardonable acts of a slave owner – splitting up a family" (p. 47). Artiste was the brother of the two hand-maidens, but his grandmother had never mentioned him.

When Stingo meets Nathan in that traumatic first encounter outside his door, Nathan has already been told by Morris Fink that Stingo is a Southerner, and Nathan uses that to taunt and jeer at him: "Too bad I won't be around for a lively conversation. [...] We could have talked about sports, I mean Southern sports like lynching niggers" (p. 69).

The following day, having apologised to Stingo and invited him to go with him and Sophie to Coney Island, Nathan has a sudden mood swing and starts taunting him again, bringing up a terrible incident that had occurred just that year, when a character called Bobby Weed was tortured and murdered by white supremacists. Nathan draws a parallel between the white Southern Americans and the Nazis during the rule of Adolf Hitler (p. 97). Stingo is furious:

> "What happened to Bobby Weed, Nathan ... was horrible, unspeakable! But I don't see any point in trying to equate one evil with another on some stupid scale of values. They're both awful! [...] I'm not one of those pigs, those troglodytes, who did what they did to Bobby Weed!" (ibid.)

Guilt is a thread that runs right through this novel: the guilt of Stingo's great-grandfather because of what had happened to Artiste; Sophie's guilt because she could not save her children and had collaborated, as she saw it, with the camp Commandant; the guilt felt by Nathan, whose remorse after one of the beatings he inflicts on Sophie sees him crying in her lap (p. 85). Stingo too feels guilt, as he thinks that he should not have left the couple and gone to South Carolina (pp. 569-70), and also that had he returned to Brooklyn immediately after he realised Sophie had left the hotel, he might have saved her.

Sophie and Nathan are buried side by side, and at their funeral Stingo reads a poem by Emily Dickinson, remembering that it was a book of her poetry that Sophie was looking for the day she first met Nathan in the Brooklyn College Library. He chose one he thought appropriate: "Ample make this bed/Make this bed with awe/In it wait till judgement break/Excellent and fair" (p. 679).

## COUNTERPOINT

In the light of the serious issues with which this novel is dealing, the inclusion of Stingo's sexual frustration as a recurring theme can seem incongruous. Some scenes, such as his encounter with Leslie Lapidus, who was eager to talk about sex but not to actually indulge in it, have an element of farce (pp. 233-243). The narrator explains, however, why he included it in the novel:

> "These many years later I am able to see how Leslie's recalcitrance – indeed her whole unassailable virginity – was a nice counterpoint to the larger narrative I have felt compelled to narrate" (p. 241)

Stingo is still a virgin at the time of his sexual encounter with Sophie in the penultimate chapter, an encounter which fulfilled all his youthful fantasies but which he will later see as a "frantic, orgiastic attempt to beat off death" (p. 658).

# FURTHER REFLECTION

## SOME QUESTIONS TO THINK ABOUT...

- What do you think of the statement: "[it is not clear] that those who were not themselves fully involved should touch upon these tragedies unscathed", (George Steiner, quoted by Stingo, p. 292). Do you think it is necessary to experience something yourself before you can write about it? Give reasons for your answer.
- Stingo experienced "a shock of recognition" when he read George Steiner's insights on the "time relation" (p. 289), that is the realisation that two vastly different experiences are taking place at precisely the same moment. Can you think of a time when you can remember exactly where you were and what you were doing at the same moment a disturbing world event was taking place? What do you think of Steiner's speculation that there are "different species of time in the same world, "good time" and enveloping folds of inhuman time, in which men fall into the hands of the living damnation" (p. 290)?

- Given Sophie is a survivor of Auschwitz, what do you think of the author's decision to create her as a gentile rather than a Jew? Give reasons for your answer.
- After reading the novel, did you feel you knew more about the Holocaust and/or slavery in the American South than you did before? Think of some specific events or moments that came as a surprise to you.
- What do you think about Stingo's decision to tell Morris Fink not to call the police, when he saw that Nathan had "gone off his trolley again" and tried to kill Sophie? (p. 582). Should Morris Fink have ignored him and called the police anyway? What do you think would have happened if he had?
- Do you think that the final tragedy was inevitable? Give reasons for your answer.
- Sophie seems to be an object of lust for the men (and some women) whose paths she crosses. Her beauty is clearly a factor in that. Do you think the author's decision to make her a beautiful and sexually attractive woman could be seen as sexist? Does her beauty help her gain the reader's sympathy or is it irrelevant? Give reasons for your answer.

- What role do you think Stingo's self-confessed lust problem has in the novel? Do you think it is an unnecessary distraction from more serious issues? Give reasons.

*We want to hear from you!
Leave a comment on your online library
and share your favourite books on social media!*

# FURTHER READING

## REFERENCE EDITION

- Styron, W. (1980) *Sophie's Choice*. London: Corgi.

## REFERENCE STUDIES

- Lynch, H. (2019) African Americans. *Britannica.com*. [Online]. [Accessed 31 March 2019]. Available from: <https://www.britannica.com/topic/African-American>

- Pallardy, R. (2019) William Styron. *Britannica.com*. [Online]. [Accessed 31 March 2019]. Available from: <https://www.britannica.com/biography/William-Styron>

- The Editors of Encyclopaedia Britannica (2019) Elie Wiesel. *Britannica.com*. [Online]. [Accessed 31 March 2019]. Available from: <https://www.britannica.com/biography/Elie-Wiesel>

- The Editors of Encyclopaedia Britannica (2019): World War II: German-occupied Europe. *Britannica.com*. [Online]. [Accessed 31 March 2019]. Available from: <https://www.britannica.com/event/World-War-II/German-occupied-Europe>

- United States Holocaust Memorial Museum (2019) *Documenting numbers of victims of the Holocaust and Nazi persecution, Key facts.* [Online]. [Accessed 1 April 2019]. Available from: <https://encyclopedia.ushmm.org/content/en/article/documenting-numbers-of-victims-of-the-holocaust-and-nazi-persecution>

## ADAPTATIONS

- *Sophie's Choice.* (1982) [Film]. Alan J. Pacula. Dir. USA: Universal Pictures.

# Bright ≡Summaries.com

## More guides to rediscover your love of literature

- *Animal Farm* by George Orwell
- *The Stranger* by Albert Camus
- *Harry Potter and the Sorcerer's Stone* by J.K. Rowling
- *The Silence of the Sea* by Vercors
- *Antigone* by Jean Anouilh
- *The Flowers of Evil* by Baudelaire

www.brightsummaries.com

Although the editor makes every effort to verify the accuracy of the information published, BrightSummaries.com accepts no responsibility for the content of this book.

© **BrightSummaries.com, 2019. All rights reserved.**

www.brightsummaries.com

Ebook EAN: 9782808019897

Paperback EAN: 9782808019903

Legal Deposit: D/2019/12603/159

Cover: © Primento

Digital conception by Primento, the digital partner of publishers.